Language Bu...

Patrick and Paula Learn about
PREPOSITIONS

by Megan Atwood
illustrated by Sole Otero

Content Consultant
Roxanne Owens
Associate Professor, Elementary Reading
DePaul University

NORWOOD HOUSE ★ PRESS
CHICAGO, ILLINOIS

Norwood House Press
P.O. Box 316598
Chicago, Illinois 60631
For information regarding Norwood House Press, please visit
our website at:
www.norwoodhousepress.com or call 866-565-2900.

Editor: Arnold Ringstad
Designer: Jake Nordby
Project Management: Red Line Editorial

Paperback ISBN: 978-1-60357-708-3

The Library of Congress has cataloged the original hardcover
edition with the following call number: 2014030274

Manufactured in the United States of America in North
Mankato, Minnesota.
262N—122014

Words in **black bold** are defined in the glossary.

Where and When

My cousin Patrick came over to my house yesterday and we had so much fun! We played hide-and-seek with my friends from school. Patrick is one year younger than me, but I still like playing with him. He loves it when I teach him things I'm learning at school. We learned all about **prepositions** in class today.

Our teacher, Ms. Katsu, told us prepositions are words that tell us where we are in time and place. When Patrick came over, we ran right to the park near my house. It's the best place for hide-and-seek. My friends and I used the game to teach Patrick all about prepositions. I think he had a lot of fun.

By Paula, age 10

"Hey Patrick," Paula said as she opened the door to the kitchen. Her cousin, Patrick, was sitting at the table.

"Hey Paula!" Patrick smiled.

"I have an awesome idea," Paula said as she threw her backpack down. "Do you want to go play hide-and-seek with my friends at the park? My dad said we could."

Patrick jumped up. "Yeah!"

"Good," she said. "Because I have a great lesson from school today! Hide-and-seek will be the perfect way to show it. Come on!"

5

Paula ran out the door, and Patrick followed right behind. They sprinted to the park and then walked over to the swing set.

"So what did you learn in school today?" Patrick asked.

Paula sat on a swing. "We learned about prepositions. They are locator words in a sentence. That means they tell you the when and where."

Patrick crinkled up his nose. "I know where I am! Why would I need a preposition?" he asked.

Paula laughed. Just then, her three friends, Sofia, Megan, and Marcus, ran up to the swings.

Paula said, "Everybody, this is my cousin, Patrick. Patrick, this is Sofia, Megan, and Marcus. They're a few grades above me. They know a lot about prepositions, and they can help you learn, too."

Marcus hopped onto a swing and rocked back and forth.

"I thought we'd play hide-and-seek and teach him," Paula said.

Megan said, "I'm wearing glasses *on* my face! That's a preposition right there!" Marcus bounced out of the swing and said, "Let's go find some more!"

Paula, Megan, Sofia, and Marcus looked at each other. Then they all yelled, "Not it!" Patrick laughed. "I guess I'm it!" he said.

Everyone but Patrick ran away. Patrick closed his eyes and counted to ten. "Ready or not, here I come!" he shouted.

When he looked up, he saw a black shoe behind a tree. He ran to the tree and reached around to poke the person standing behind it. It was Paula.

"Shoot!" Paula said and laughed. She added, "I thought I'd be safe behind this tree." She turned to Patrick and asked, "Did you hear the preposition in that sentence? It was *behind*. It told you where I was. *Behind* is an example of a preposition of place. Those are prepositions that let you know where things are. Can you think of any others?"

Patrick thought for a moment. "What about *under* and *in*?" he asked.

"Yep, that's right!" Paula replied. She added, "Maybe you should have counted for more than a minute!" Then she said, "Hey! I just used a preposition for time."

Patrick asked, "Which word was the preposition?"

"*For*," Paula replied. "I said 'for more than a minute.' Prepositions of time help tell you when things happen or how long they take. I could have also said, 'You've been counting since I left you.' The word *since* is another preposition of time."

Patrick nodded. Paula said, "Prepositions can do lots of other things too. Let's go find everyone else together. Along the way, we'll use different prepositions."

"Sounds good!" said Patrick. "Let's walk toward those trees."

Paula said, "There's another one: *toward*! This preposition talks about moving somewhere. Another one like this is *to*. Guess what else I used? A **prepositional phrase**."

Patrick asked, "What's that?"

Paula pointed to a shrub where a long ponytail was sticking out. She and Patrick laughed and walked over to it. Paula whispered, "A prepositional phrase is a series of words that starts with a preposition such as, 'toward those trees.'"

Paula and Patrick reached the shrub then stepped around it fast. They yelled, "Boo!"

Megan shrieked. "I wasn't expecting both of you!" she said, laughing.

Paula couldn't stop laughing either. "You had the best look on your face!"

Then Megan stopped. "Hey, we just used prepositions of place. You said the look was *on* my face. That tells us where the look was."

Paula said, "Other prepositions of place are *at* or *in*. We are *at* the park. We are hiding *in* the woods. See? All of those are prepositional phrases. "

Patrick asked, "Is *around* another preposition about place?" Paula nodded. Patrick smiled and pointed to another tree. "I see a green tennis shoe back there. Let's sneak *around* that tree!"

Megan said, "That's Marcus! Let's go get him."

Paula, Patrick, and Megan tiptoed toward
the distant tree. Right before they got there,
Marcus jumped out.

"Boo!" he yelled. Marcus laughed.
"I could hear you guys talking from all the
way over here."

Megan turned to Patrick. "Did you catch that preposition, Patrick?"

Patrick thought for a moment. "Was it *from*? That told us where Marcus heard us."

Megan responded, "That's right!"

Marcus said, "Actually, I'm really glad you found me. I don't know where Sofia is. Let's all look together. We can talk about even more prepositions."

Paula said, "Good idea! I'll start. I wonder if Sofia walked over that bridge." She pointed to a small bridge that went over a creek.

Megan said, "Good idea! Patrick, the word *over* is a preposition. So is *under*."

Marcus started walking. "Yeah, but she probably wouldn't hide under the bridge. She'd get her feet wet!"

Patrick laughed. "I think I might be getting it." Then he looked around. "I wonder where she's at?"

Megan, Marcus, and Paula looked at each other. Paula said, "You just used a preposition at the end of a sentence."

Patrick looked confused. "Can't you do that?"

Paula shrugged. "It's okay sometimes, but our teacher said if you can avoid it, you should."

Megan nodded. "Yeah, so in your sentence, you didn't even need the preposition *at*. You could have just said . . ."

Marcus jumped in, "I wonder where she is!"

Patrick's eyes went wide. "So most of the time, prepositions need something after them. Something has to complete the prepositional phrase."

Suddenly, they heard giggling behind them. "I caught you guys!" Sofia said. Then she shook her wet foot. "I was under the bridge." She looked at Patrick. "Do you know which word was the preposition?"

Patrick said proudly, "It was *under,* and *under the bridge* is the prepositional phrase!"

Sofia smiled. "Wow! You've learned a lot!"

Marcus said, "I think there's only one more thing to learn. We can't forget to talk about the **object of the preposition**."

Megan nodded excitedly. "Yeah! Most prepositions have to have an object at the end of their phrase. It's normally a noun."

Patrick nodded slowly. "I know that a noun is a person, place, or thing. So . . ." He jumped up and shot his fist in the air. "The object of the preposition in the prepositional phrase *under the bridge* is *bridge*!"

Paula asked, "What would the object be in my hiding spot, *behind the tree*?"

Patrick replied right away, "*Tree*!"

Megan, Sofia, Marcus, and Paula all whooped. "You got it!" yelled Marcus.

Paula looked up and noticed the sun was starting to go down. "We should probably go. Thanks so much for playing with us!"

Patrick said, "I learned a lot about prepositions today. Thank you so much!"

Everybody laughed and said their goodbyes. Paula and Patrick started walking home. Paula said, "Should we review on our way home? What did you learn?"

Patrick said, "I learned that a preposition is a word that tells you where and when things are. I also learned they normally have other words around them. This is the object of the preposition. Together, prepositions and objects make up prepositional phrases."

Paula stopped in her tracks. "Exactly! You know, you're pretty smart. No wonder we're related."

They both grinned at each other and ran the rest of the way home.

Know Your Prepositions

Prepositions tell where and when things are. Sentences don't need to have prepositions, but they can make your sentences clearer. Compare the following two sentences. "He hid." "He hid behind the tall tree." The prepositional phrase gives you extra information.

Some prepositions that tell you where things are include *at, in, against, below, with*, and *between*. There are many more like this. Time prepositions include *before, after*, and *since*.

Prepositions aren't used alone. They need to be part of prepositional phrases. You can't just say, "I played video games after." You need to complete the phrase. You could say, "I played video games after school," or "I played video games after doing homework." In these examples, the prepositional phrases are *after school* and *after doing homework*.

Find the prepositions in these sentences. After you find them, figure out what the prepositional phrases are. There may be more than one prepositional phrase in some sentences!

He only counted for 60 seconds.

Megan had a scared look on her face.

The kids went toward the yellow color behind a tree.

Patrick looked behind trees, beside rocks, near the playground, and underneath bushes.

Writing Activity

Prepositional phrases can add a lot of information to a sentence. Think about the sentence, "I ran." You could make it a lot more interesting with prepositional phrases. "I ran to the finish line of the race at the school on Sunday."

Write a few simple sentences. Then, add some prepositional phrases to make the sentences more interesting and add more information. How many prepositional phrases can you use in a single sentence?

Glossary

object of the preposition: the words after a preposition in a prepositional phrase.

prepositions: words that describe how words in a sentence relate to each other. They may show a time or a place relationship.

prepositional phrase: a group of words that work together to show a time or place relationship.

For More Information

Books

Ganeri, Anita. *Describing Words: Adjectives, Adverbs, and Prepositions*. Chicago: Heinemann Library, 2012.

Time for Kids: Grammar Rules!. New York: Time Home Entertainment, 2013.

Websites

List of Prepositions
http://www.towson.edu/ows/prepositions.htm
This website has a list of more than 50 prepositions. It also has examples of different kinds of prepositional phrases.

Prepositions Game
http://www.angles365.com/classroom/fitxers/6e/catmouse.swf
Play this game to practice your preposition skills.

About the Author

Megan Atwood is a freelance writer and editor in Minneapolis, MN. She has two cats named Albie and Genevieve.